Abo
PORTH

by
Tony Roberts

Illustrations
by
Elizabeth Roberts

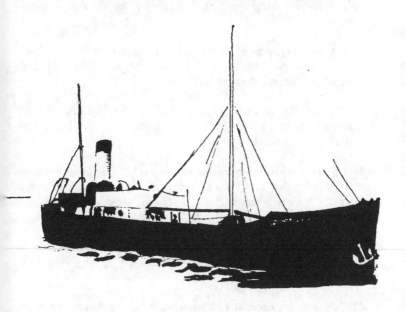

Abercastle Publications

Abercastle Publications

Guide to the Pembrokeshire Coast Path by Tony Roberts. Sketch maps and illustrations by Elizabeth Roberts. The complete Coast Path is conveniently sectioned with distances, times and degree of difficulty. Plus a wealth of other information.

Try the Best Walks in Pembrokeshire by Tony Roberts. With maps and illustrations by Elizabeth Roberts. A range of different walks – on the coast, over the Preseli mountains, through woodland and around towns.

The Geology of Pembrokeshire by Dr. Brian S. John. The diverse and complicated geology of this area, which has played such an important part in shaping the history of the county, is clearly explained.

Myths and Legends of Pembrokeshire retold by Tony Roberts. Stories from the Mabinogion, sightings of mermaids, the little people, phantoms, corpse candles . . .

St. Davids (Tŷ Ddewi) by Tony Roberts. Explore the city, the cathedral, the coast path and beaches in the area. Read about the history and folk tales.

Welsh Herbal Medicine by David Hoffman. "This small book is a brief look at the wisdom and practices of the old physicians of Wales". History, legends and a description and use of the most common medicinally used plants.

Myths and Legends of Wales retold by Tony Roberts. Tales from the Mabinogion, about Arthur, Saints, Mermaids, Witches, the Little People, Phantoms . . .

1797 French Invasion at Fishguard/Glaniad y Ffrancod yn Abergwaun. By Tony Roberts. A short history of the French Invasion. Bilingual. Illustrated by Royston Hopson and Elizabeth Roberts.

Contents

The North Pembrokeshire Coast 4

The Village of Porthgain 5

Geology 6

History 7

Architecture 10

An Account of Stone-Crushing 12

Lime and its Importance 19

Other Villages 20

The Antiquities 24

Walking 26

Folklore and the Early Celtic Saints 30

5th issue (Revised)
© 1991 E. A. Roberts
Published by Abercastle Publications, 2002.
Waunblaen, Felinwynt, Aberteifi, Ceredigion, SA43 1RW
Printed by Dinefwr Press, Llandybïe, Carmarthenshire

The North Pembrokeshire Coast

From Strumble Head down to St David's Head the rock-bound coast is possibly the most beautiful in Britain; but to seamen it has always been dangerous and inhospitable.

Nowadays it is a middle-class playground, the unspoilt pride of the National Park, protected from development by the National Park Authority.

But the coast was once studded with small ports serving their local community. They lasted until after the First World War, though the coming of the railways hit them hard. Despite the dangers of navigating along such a rock-bound coast, there has been constant trade since earliest times. Neolithic man may even have come by sea – certainly three thousand years ago, there was Bronze Age trade with Ireland; and the early Celtic Saints of 500 A.D. made long and hazardous sea voyages in their frail craft between here and France and Ireland.

Abercastle, just to the north of Porthgain, and Porth Clais, the harbour for St David's, were thriving little ports before Elizabethan times. And the existence of so many lime kilns in Pembrokeshire coastal villages testifies to the constant coming and going of little sailing ships with cargoes of limestone and coal from the south of the county and the Cleddau ports, for the acid fields of the north.

The other small ports of north Pembrokeshire – St Dogmael's, Newport, Fishguard, Solva – all had their moments of greatness and have now relapsed, mostly into tourist centres. Porthgain owed its growth, a "mushroom" one in that there was no village in early Victorian times, solely to the quarrying, first of slates and then of roadstone, granite if you like, with brick-making as an ancillary occupation.

Unlike some once flourishing coastal villages, it is a very living community still – while it is a lot more crowded in the summer, it does not depend for its existence on the second-home industry.

This is a very Welsh community: in the summer, the pub is full of English visitors, but in the winter, Welsh is the normal language.

The Village of Porthgain

Porthgain is a small hamlet in the parish of Llanrhian half-way along the coast between Strumble Head and St David's.

It consists of a miscellaneous group of houses on a hillside, a pub, a wide dusty space, once green in the middle, an art gallery on the left, a cafe in *Tŷ Mawr*, the harbour ahead and the tall brick ruins on the west side of the harbour. Also boat trips with a local fisherman.

For those who know it, Porthgain is one of the most individual places in Pembrokeshire. With its genuine unpretentiousness and really superb coastal scenery and walking, it offers more simple and satisfying pleasures than almost anywhere else in the county.

That is the village today but in the busy days of Edwardian England, the quarry would be turning out some 40,000 tons of stone and chippings annually for the roads of Britain. In addition, there was brick-making and, previously, slate quarrying.

The most prominent feature, the ruined storage bins have, like all ruins, a timeless air, especially when moonlight and bad weather tinge them with an almost tragic grandeur.

There are few living in the village today who remember the windows closed against the dust, the noise of the crusher and the engines, the trucks full of stone and the ships tied up alongside the quays, the bustle of the engine sheds and repair shops. For the quarry only closed in 1931 and though trade was never really good in the Twenties, yet there was constant activity in the harbour, both sailing and steam vessels loading and some sixty or seventy men constantly employed.

Geology

Here, a note on the geology around Porthgain seems appropriate since in a quarrying district, geology is all-important. All the rocks of this area are very old, mainly Ordovician, dating back in geological time some 400 million years. These are both igneous and sedimentary rocks.

Igneous rocks are of the earth's basic material coming from the interior of the earth by volcanic activity. Extrusive are those which cool on the surface, while Intrusive are cooled inside the earth. Sedimentary rocks are laid down in layers in water over long, long periods and turned into rocks by pressure.

Like other places along the coast, the headlands at Porthgain are the tremendously hard igneous rocks which have resisted erosion; and the bay is of softer sedimentary rocks. Round the harbour these are dark-coloured sandy mudstones, interbedded with sandstones.

Didymograptus Fossils

From a geological point of view, Abereiddi is regarded as of greater interest. It is the best known locality for Ordovician rocks eroded into softer Llanvirn shales, the name for the formation being taken from the farm at the west of the bay. The western end of the beach is where the famous "tuning fork" graptolites are found in the pieces of shale.

The stone quarried at Porthgain is described geologically as a dolerite intrusion in the Ordovician sediment, medium to fine grain in texture and an attractive blue-grey in colour. It is very hard and is exceptionally fine as a roadstone. Trwyncastell to the north is rhyolite lava.

History

The early Ordnance Survey maps do not even show a roadway, though doubtless a few fishermen kept their boats there and The Sloop Inn probably dates from pre-Ordnance Survey times.

The industrial history would appear to have begun in 1837, George LeHunte of Artramont, County Wexford in Ireland, and of St Botolph's near Milford, granted a lease to extract slates, flags and stones. The LeHuntes came to inherit such a disparate group of properties through marriage into the Lloyd family of Cilciffeth. The Artramont Arms in Croesgoch is named after their seat in County Wexford, but these Lords of the Manor of Llanrhian were not farmers or great landowners and found the need for raising money at times. The mining lease covered two fields of the "Island of Barry, Llanryan", a farm of 500 acres then farmed by James Morgan. The lease was granted to W. J. Ward of St David's, J. Jones of Trefin and E. Williams of Fishguard. This was surrendered several times, notably 1839 and 1841 before another was granted in 1949 to Benjamin Haill, Robert Norman and John Barclay, all of London. Thus in 10 years, the original local operators were replaced by a consortium "from away". And so, in fact, the Company remained, an English one until operations ceased in 1931. There were several changes of name:

London Crushed Stone, United Stone Firms of Bristol, and Porthgain Village Industries, a subsidiary first of General Refractories and now of G. R. Stein Refractories of Sheffield.

The Company retained the mineral rights and owned the ruined hoppers and crushing plant, the harbour, the land in the centre of the village and much of the property. Porthgain was entirely a "Company" village, all employment being dependent on the prosperity of the quarry; the atmosphere was paternal and everything in the records suggests that the Company was a good employer. Apart from farming, it offered almost the only work in the area and spartan though Victorian living conditions were in this remote part of Britain, people undoubtedly lived a better life than in the large cities.

There are no complete records of output annually, or indeed any records of the early slate-quarrying and brick-making, so it is possible only to build up a picture based on those statistics available.

Porthgain is an interesting example of a self-contained industrial development using local resources.

Slate was quarried both at Porthgain and at Abereiddi but on a smaller scale than at the other major Pembrokeshire quarries. Of these, only Llangolman still produces slate at the present time, an attractive olive-green colour compared with the blue-grey of Glogue, the blue-black of Rosebush. The Abereiddi slates were not of the finest quality. Technically their cleavage was inferior especially compared with Caernarvon, and this meant more wastage. They were also too absorbant. The geologists maintain that the absence of full metamorphosis is the reason for the unfavourably comparison with Caernarvon slate.

It is not known how early the slate quarries were worked. Many quarries were worked all over the county to provide slates for domestic use; there are several in the Porthgain area, all now disused. The mineral rights were granted before 1840 and slates were exported for over 50 years although on a small scale.

The bricks were made from the crushed slate shale; the crusher and bins were built; stone was quarried and exported. The slates and bricks were little more than for local use; the road-stone was another matter and was exported on a quite large scale before it too ceased, leaving the empty buildings and disused machinery. The latter was sold off and the buildings gradually deteriorated into the skeletons they are today. They were listed as derelict buildings suitable for demolition until the Welsh Office scheduled them as worthy of preservation.

Of the buildings in the village, only the finely built stone machinery shed, Tŷ Mawr, remains. The brick-drying sheds and the brick-making shed have disappeared and the workshops are derelict. The tall chimneys were demolished in 1954.

On the top of the cliff, the numerous sheds and some cottages have virtually disappeared. Of the elaborate railway system, nothing now remains except a few bits of sleeper and rail. The small pilot hut remains by the steep steps to the cliffs. There were water wheels and a leat which ran down by the cottages, but even the latter is barely traceable except from the top, though it discharges effectively enough below the quay.

To the right of the harbour, above the stile, the natural contour is obscured by a hill which is in fact a huge mound of spoil. This was removed from the harbour and hauled up by traction engine.

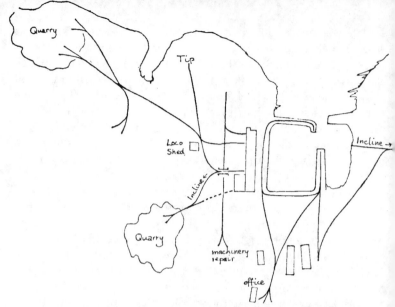

On the cliffs too, to the seaward side of the main slate quarry, the headland has been changed by the enormous quantity of slate waste.

The harbour itself, as we know it, is man-made about the middle of last century. It was re-built with larger quays between 1902 and 1904 and in the years that followed, the improvements were reflected by increased shipping activities. Even as late as 1930 an additional improvement was made, the quay being shortened to allow a hoped-for 170 ft 650 ton ship to enter. The harbour dries out completely at Low Water; and at High Water draws 13 ft at the quay and 16 ft at the entrance. The depth is a couple of feet less at the moment, because of silting.

Architecture

The buildings of Porthgain are neither beautilul nor picturesque. The houses are a hotch-potch of traditional, Victorian and later styles, of largely indeterminate age and a few modern bungalows built now to a very strict specification of the National Park Committee, though looking aesthetically little more attractive for it.

The pièce de résistance is undoubtedly the Street, the row of cottages facing the village. There are five of them, all lived in but the last of which has lost its roof. The rooms are all good-sized and comfortable and certainly disprove the contention of those who say that old cottages are insanitary and inferior to council houses. These cottages are scheduled as worthy of preservation.

The restaurant was formerly the Company's offices; modern rendering and windows hide any signs of period or style. But the most interesting feature about the village is that there are few houses which are not lived, in full-time by residents; the secondhome industry has made no headway here. It is an honest-to-goodness working village with plain houses in the Welsh style. Although there is no bus service, most people living in the village have access to private transport to do their shopping in Haverfordwest and Fishguard.

The Sloop Inn is a convivial centre and became well-known throughout the county for its sing-songs.

A few new houses have been built but in general it has become pretty well impossible to get permission to develop in any way.

An Account of Stone-crushing

In 1909 Bristol took 25 shipments in three months, in all some 3,500 tons. In the same period, Newhaven took 4,000 tons in 18 shipments and the same tonnage went to local ports, mainly Haverfordwest, Neyland and Milford, or rather Castle Pill, for there were no docks then. Other shipments went to Barnstaple, Bridgewater, Braunton, Newport (Mon.), Minehead and, further afield, to London and Whitstable. In this three months, there were over 100 sailings. This was by no means exceptional, sometimes ships queued up waiting.

In the 19th century they were mainly sailing vessels, ketches, schooners and later steamships too. The Company itself built six special ships for carrying the crushed stone, of 350 tons each. In fact, sailing vessels continued after the First War even.

Local destinations in one year, 1910 taken as an example, were to Cardigan, Fishguard, Abercastle, Aberaeron, St David's, Haverfordwest, Solva, Neyland, St Bride's, Pwllgwaelod, Ceibwr, Tresaith, and Aberporth. It is noticeable that many of these harbours had no quay to come alongside, so the vessels must have been beached, unloaded and refloated on the next tide: the same old-fashioned way lime and culm were handled.

Further afield, roadstone went to Dublin, Cork and Belfast as well as the ports mentioned earlier. Llanelli too had a cargo of bricks.

It was a very specialised trade. Unlike Abercastle which exported grain and butter and took in general merchandise, Porthgain took nothing but coal for its own use. Most ships in fact came in light or in ballast. Typical recorded movements were: Bessie, light from St David's (that is, Porth Clais), left for Neyland with granite; the Porthgain, from Kinlochleven with timber (presumably for repairs or re-building) with granite for Bristol; Calatum, light from Cardiff to Newhaven with granite.

There would be much less trade in winter, or when the weather was bad; sometimes a ship would be unable to enter – imagine bringing a sailing vessel, or even a steamship of two to three hundred tons, in such a narrow entrance with a following sea!

By 1930 though, the bins were full, ships were few and far between, but there was expectation of a large ship for the South Coast trade; silted up sand and rock was shifted from the harbour floor. The bins were reorganised and the quay shortened to allow a 650-tonner to enter. But the manager who chafed under the inactivity and worked desperately hard to keep the quarry going was warned not to carry any unnecessary men.

The method of quarrying was to put a small charge in a drilled hole; the resultant shattered rock can be seen in numerous places in the quarry bottom. A larger charge of black powder, gunpowder, then blew up large pieces of rock which would then be reduced. When the rock was crushed it would be sent into the hopper of the appropriate size, ranging from dust up to 3" stone.

Ships tied up alongside would be loaded from the hoppers close by, entering under their own steam or being warped in.

There was an elaborate system of railways or tramways, with little trucks or skips into which material would be loaded. In addition to the engines which pulled the trucks, there were traction engines for pulling the trucks up the inclines.

There were two parts to the railway system, an upper serving the quarries and a lower along the quays. The top railways ran along the cliffs too for half a mile to the quarries, and there was an elaborate network connecting quarries, crushing plant and waste tip. Some of the quarry workings were connected by a cable operated incline, with an Avel and Porter single cylinder traction working it. Another incline was used to bring raw slate from the slate quarry to the preparation plant behind the locomotive shed.

The quayside network was to help load ships and to discharge ballast. A long tunnel gave access to the slate quarry and was used for the removal of some waste. It was used too for bringing out shale for brick-making. On the east side of the harbour a little line connected to the quayside lines and was used to clean out the silted sand. At the top of a short incline leading down to the water was an old Wallis and Stevens traction engine to haul up. At Low Water trucks were loaded with ballast jettisoned from

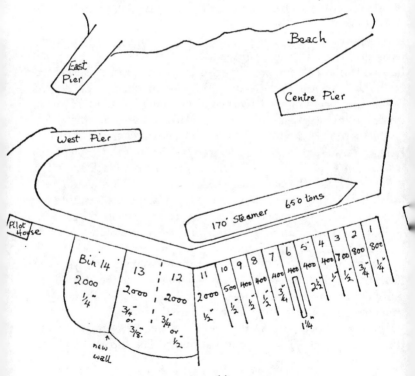

14

ships, and also the sand to be removed from the seaward end of the harbour.

Horses seem to have been used at first on both levels. The original locomotive appears to have been the Porthgain, a wing tank Barclay engine. A second locomotive came about 1919. A third engine, 311, eventually replaced the Porthgain. A traction engine, 7273 was used to haul wagons with stone to Mathry Road station.

Records of activity are uneven: they are lacking for the earliest periods of quarrying, and although abundant, they are incomplete after the turn of the century.

The busiest years were those of the First World War and just before. In the 20s trade slackened, as it did all over Britain in the days of the Slump. Orders would be low, no boats would come day after day, and all the traffic would be that of local lorries. The men would be quarrying and crushing, transporting and maintaining machinery. Perhaps one or two boats a week would come. The ketch Portland would take chippings to Saundersfoot; S/S Ben Rein would take 150 tons of macadam to Bristol.

By 1929 trade was low; much woodwork was decayed and repairs were needed on the crusher. The harbour silted up badly. Men had to be employed removing the sand. There might still be up to 60 men working on breaking, crushing and transporting, though output was down to less than 200 tons a day.

In summer, trade would pick up; the Ben Rein would be

leaving for Saundersfoot and Neyland, Agnes for Braunton, Claire May for Pembroke, Delorain for Bristol, m.v. Traly for Bridgewater and Bessie for Braunton.

Operations were controlled by a Roadstone Controller at Bristol who kept an overall eye on policy, and a local manager controlled the day-to-day operations; for most of the First War and Post-War period these were Captain MacIntosh as Controller and Mr Crone the local manager. The latter was Irish and is remembered as a fine engineer; he certainly looked most unwillingly on the decline of the fortune of the quarry. Records do not show that more than about 75 men were employed and these included those who worked in the quarries, the crushing plant, transporting; and the craftsmen – engineers, smith, pilot and so on. Output varied of course, a good week producing about 1,000 tons but perhaps half that would be more normal. Wages were low but compared favourably with what could be earned on a farm, the only alternative employment. Those who lived in a Company house paid little rent, 10d. a week for a cottage. The cottages were in fact condemned in 1939 but their demolition was fortunately postponed for the duration. Most of the men who worked in the quarries came from Trefin as well as Porthgain, and some came from St David's.

In 1929, United Stone Firms came under a Receivership; there were still some shipments to Bristol, Devon, and local County Council orders. An individual ship might take 200 tons at a time but this did little to keep the quarry working and there was a limit to the amount of maintenance work and repairs.

The manager did his best to fight a delaying action when it came to removing equipment to others of the Company's quarries, and to dismantling the installations; but the writing was on the wall. Trade dwindled away to individual lorry loads through the thirties and forties.

Nonetheless, in the very comprehensive County Development Plan drawn up after the War, Mr J. A. Price stated that Porthgain should, in the event of high quality roadstone being needed in the future, be regarded as the best quarry to re-open. But in view of the emphasis placed on amenity these days, it is somewhat unlikely that the National Park Committee would sanction this, even if the harbour and village itself were left alone.

Industrial archaeology has achieved fairly recent popularity, and Pembrokeshire has much to offer to devotees: practically all its industries are in the past.

Quarrying gets a bad press these days, especially in National Parks, since these institutions have two mutually contradictory terms of reference. These are to try and keep wild and beautiful areas as wild and beautiful as possible; and secondly to try and make as many people come and enjoy them as possible. So one of the main results from a human standpoint is that lots of people want to come and stay either for a holiday or to have a second home or retire.

This has been the fate of West Wales, and many other areas. Industrial activity, even on a local scale, is looked at askance. But with its fortunately inadequate road system and absence of railways, the Porthgain area is hardly suitable these days for a resurgence of roadstone quarrying. Thus, it is not very probable that interest a few years ago by a Kent firm in reopening the quarry, will come to anything. Though it is not certain that mineral and quarrying rights have been extinguished.

But a more subtle threat appeared in 1990 when a self-styled conservationist proposed to develop a group of houses or apartments, in the ruins, as holiday homes. How this could be physically achieved without changing the outlines or without setting up a community of troglodytes has yet to be explained. The National Park Officer gave the developer permission to go ahead and produce a feasibility study. The official attitude was apparently softened by the promise that an Information arid Interpretive Centre, Community Hall, Craft Shop, and Exhibition Hall might be provided – in other words, all those features that turn living communities into tourist theme parks. Local reaction was sceptical, especially when the developer was featured in a colourful and derogatory article in the *News of the World*.

Tŷ Mawr, the old machinery shed in the centre, has now been re-roofed and made safe and watertight by the National Park Authority. There has been a lot of interest (and concern) about its future use and a number of proposals put forward. At the moment there are two serious contenders and a decision should be imminent. The lean-to on the side is a cafe and booking place for the boat trips.

Lime and its Importance

Just past the Sloop and before the slipway is a large round stone lime-kiln, now restored and now scheduled as worthy of preservation, an honour not yet accorded to the many old farmhouses in the county.

In the 19th century there were some three dozen working limekilns in North Pembrokeshire – and many more in the South of the county. Their use is recorded at St David's as early as 1384.

The acid soils of the county have a great need of lime to sweeten them. Up to the end of the Victorian age culm and lime ships were a regular feature of the trading landscape of Pembrokeshire. Gradually the system of railway and later road delivery superseded the sea.

Lime was brought as crushed limestone from the quarries in the south of the county, notably from West Williamston on the Cleddau estuary. The culm was anthracite dust and shattered coal. It was exported from places like Hook, or Saundersfoot, possibly Nolton Haven. This culm, mixed with clay and made into briquettes was the widely used domestic fuel until quite recently.

Almost every small haven in the north-west had its lime-kiln. The little ships would be beached, unloaded and refloated on the tide.

Inside the kiln, a fire would be lit, with layers of culm and limestone, put in from the top. The quick-lime resulting from the burning would be pushed out, and since the fuel was anthracite, there would be no coke mixed with it. The quick-lime would be slaked nearby, and then carted to the fields.

The round kilns, sometimes they might be square as at Caerbwdi, were called pot-kilns and they were unlined, unlike the larger draw-kilns which were lined with fire-brick and kept continuously burning. Pot-kilns needed 7 to 10 cwt of culm to produce a ton of lime. Nowadays lime is supplied in bulk and the kilns remain as interesting survivals of a past maritime way of life.

Other Villages

Adjacent to Porthgain and associated with it industrially, is Abereiddi, a small hamlet a couple of miles to the west. Little now remains of it since the cottages in the centre are nearly all second homes and to the east, the cottages and buildings formerly connected with the slate quarrying are heaps of rubble. Belatedly, the remaining cottages are now scheduled as worthy of preservation.

Although privately owned, the land on the shore forms an excellent car park. After a particularly heavy storm in 1974, the County Council built a sea wall.

As we have noted, geologists find Abereiddi specially interesting. There is little now to be seen from an industrial archaeology point of view. But the former quarry is well worth a visit. Local fishermen blasted away the rock at the seaward side, making a narrow channel and turning the quarry into a natural harbour, a splendidly sheltered one, incidentally. The water is very blue and very deep; the walls are sheer and impressive and the local name of The Blue Lagoon has achieved some fame.

From Abereiddi down to St David's there are no more villages but to the north are Aberfelin and Abercastle. Aberfelin is now no more than a ruined mill and a couple of cottages. It is the beach for Trefin, the largest neighbouring village. Trefin was a "straggling" village even in the 18th century. In the Middle Ages there was a palace of the Bishop of St David's here, a week-end place so to speak. The large farm, Longhouse, between Trefin and Abercastle, once belonged to the See of St David's as a grange, "a most excellent corn farm" as Fenton said. It now belongs to the National Trust.

Abercastle is a picturesque decayed port. A few people live there but there is no longer a pub or shop. Many houses are holiday cottages. Good fishing and sailing harbour. But in Elizabethan times it was a port; ships were even built there. The large stone granary bears witness to its standing as a port.

Fenton, writing at the end of the 18th century, noted that there were a few sloops belonging to the port. An export trade in corn and butter was carried on, returning with shop goods etc. from Bristol and Liverpool, some of the smaller craft carrying coal, culm and limestone from Milford.

Croesgoch is a cross-roads village on the A487. Much of the traffic hurtles through so fast that the nucleus of the village is barely noticed. There is a shop and Post Office, pub, artist's gallery, and a large and handsome Baptist Chapel standing back.

Apart from their functional aspects, it must be admitted that the local villages are not of major scenic or architectural interest.

The hamlet of Llanrhian consists of the Manor Farm, council houses, a closed-down school and an attractive medieval church which is a little unusual in this part of the county in having a tower at all, for most of the north Pembrokeshire churches are small and simple with a bell-cote only. The church was rebuilt in 1836 and restored in 1896. It has a stepped western gable and a low saddle-back roof. There is an unusual decagonal, or ten-sided, font; one side bears the arms, three ravens (martlets or choughs according to the historian Fenton), of Sir Rhys ap Thomas of

Carew, also of Rickeston closer by, the great supporter of Henry Tudor when he returned to become Henry VII. One of the loveliest of the simple Welsh churches is close by at Llanhowel, signposted on the A487 road to St David's. It is a most attractive setting and consists of nave, chancel and north chapel only.

Abereiddi was in fact producing – and exporting – slates before the quarries at Porthgain were developed.

The slates were exported from Porthgain harbour: a rail, or rather tram, road was built round Ynys Barri over a 3 mile distance: the platform can still be traced.

In 1981, residents bought their cottages in the street, and a couple of other houses. The National Park Authority bought the quarries, ruined bins, and other buildings, and the harbour.

More recently the National Trust have bought much of Ynys Barri, i.e. the coastland from Porthgain to Abereiddi including the industrial ruins and Blue Lagoon at Abereiddi.

The Antiquities

But much of tbe charm of this stretch of coastline lies in what can be found between the villages. Of really considerable importance are the antiquarian remains.

First in point of time is a magnificent New Stone Age cromlech or burial chamber, Carreg Samson or Long-house. More massive than Pentre Evan, even if not so elegant, it is a short distance either from the Coast Path or from the road. Between Abercastle and Trefin is Longhouse Farm and there is a public right of way from the farmyard to the monument. A more rewarding approach is from the Coast Path. Leaving Abercastle on foot, you walk past the handsome lime kiln to the valley, Cwm Badau, and a signpost directs you up the creek to the huge burial chamber above. It consists of a massive capstone some 15 ft by 9 ft and 3 to 6 ft thick, the weight carried on three supporters, between 5 to 6 ft high. It is dated at about 3,000 B.C.

Carreg Samson lies a quarter of a mile to the south-west of a small island which is itself on the north side of Abercastle. The island is accessible only at low water. The 2½" Ordnance Survey map shows an entrenchment marked Castle, but the rock formation, to the Ancient Monuments Commission, seemed natural. One mound is called, curiously, the Grave of Samson's Finger. In his official Coast Path Guide Mr John Barrett suggests that the faintly rectangular marking reminiscent of Gateholm indicates an early Christian site rather than an Iron Age fort (or the Grave of the Finger). No-one has satisfactorily explained the name Samson and whether he really put the capstone of the cromlech on with the finger which now lies a few hundred yards across the water. There are other Samson references in north Pembrokeshire, notably a burial chamber at St Nicholas. They could refer to the biblical Samson or to the 6th century holy man who was Abbot of Caldy and later became St Samson of Dol in Brittany. Either way the relationship to stone monuments which preceded both of them by a couple of thousand years is unclear. It is worth crossing to the island and climbing up, for the moment when the Burial Chamber comes into view up the Cwm.

On the Coast Path between Abercastle and Aberfelin is a fine example of a rocky headland made into an Iron Age Fort, Castell Coch. Across the promontory are two earth and stone banks. The outer rampart is some 80 ft long and the area enclosed is about three acres.

There is another Iron Age fort in the Porthgain area. This was Trwyncastell, between Porthgain and Abereiddi, out on the headland beyond the Abereiddi slate quarries. The tower is thought to be a recent, or at least nineteenth century, navigation aid.

And, getting a little out of the area, there is a large Iron Age promontory fort just before the little bay of Trepwll: reachable from the coast road by a footpath from the farm Pwllcaerog; or along the Coast Path from Abereiddi.

At the other end of our area, a couple of miles north-east of Porthgain, a little before Abermawr is a fine Iron Age fort called Castell Coch.

The Iron Age forts are a couple of thousand years nearer our time than the Stone Age burial chambers. Few of them are "forts" as such: 'defended settlements' would be a more accurate term and none of them in this area would be likely to have contained more than one extended family.

Walking

But the past – the industrial history and the antiquarian past
are only one facet; and for some people not the major one, of this
part of the county. The scenery of the coastline, the wild flowers
and the old remains, all add immensely to the interest. In
honesty, one must add that it is the coastal scenery rather than

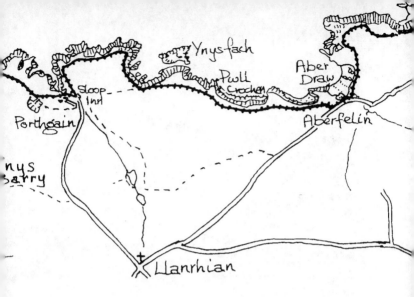

that inland which is so fine. Inland the landscape is flat and, though pleasant and unspoiled, has little of the grandeur that distinguishes the whole coastline from Fishguard to St David's.

One of Britain's most distinguished geographers described the coast between Porthgain and Abereiddi as the finest in Britain.

The walks found here are very good indeed with reasonable access and parking. Starting from Porthgain Harbour going west, it is 1.5 miles to Abereiddi, taking threequarters of an hour (depending on how often you stop to admire the view, the wild flowers, sea-birds, the quarry or whatever). The first part of the track is a bit rutted by cattle which makes for uncomfortable walking but the going is level and easy. Start by going up the steps at the Harbour.

In fact the whole Coast Path round here is pleasantly easy going and you can reckon on doing more than the 2 miles an hour which is about par for the hillier parts of the coast. On the way to Abereiddi, you can descend to Traethllwyn, one of the finest beaches anywhere. There is no car access to it except by going through Barry Island Farm, but don't get caught by the tide or sit too close under the rocks. Towards the Abereiddi end, don't miss the Blue Lagoon, the old quarry, which, as we have

said, was blasted open to make a most beautiful small harbour, even though the entrance is a bit narrow.

From Abereiddi you can walk on the Coast Path all the way to St David's Head and then on to Whitesand Bay where you pick up the road. It is a very fine walk, some five to six miles. Once past Abereiddi there is no place at which the Coast Path touches the road though it is quite close at Penberry Farm, after the first couple of miles.

The two peaks of Penberry (Penbiri) and Carn Llidi, just before St David's Head rise like mountains, though in fact they are both only about 600 ft.

There is a fine Iron Age settlement on St David's Head with a massive wall cutting off the headland and hut circles inside it. There are early Celtic field patterns visible from the summit of Carn Llidi – best seen when the bracken is gone, out of season.

North-east from Porthgain, the walking is equally fine all the way to Fishguard on the Coast Path. It's five miles to Abermawr, where the Path touches the road; and about another five to Strumble Head lighthouse: good, hard going with scenery as fine as you will find anywhere. For a shorter walk, it is a mile and a half from Porthgain to Aberfelin and another couple of miles to Abercastle. From Abercastle there is a fine walk on to Pwllstrodyr, returning by the footpath inland and by road back to Abercastle. Abercastle back to Aberfelin by road, going through Trefin and from Aberfelin back to Porthgain, you can go by road, a pleasant walk (the footpath across the field is not waymarked), or retrace your footsteps on the cliffs. Abereiddi back to Porthgain is better on the cliffs, though if you go by road you pass a fine 18th century farmhouse and buildings, Trevacoon.

Car Parking: good at Porthgain, at Abereiddi and Strumble Head and free. Good at Whitesand Bay though crowded in summer and a charge is made. There is little room for parking at Aberfelin, Abercastle and Abermawr though in summer it can be difficult.

Public lavatories at Porthgain, Abereiddi, Trefin, Whitesand and Abercastle. Telephone boxes at Porthgain, Abercastle and Trefin. Refreshments at Porthgain and Whitesand.

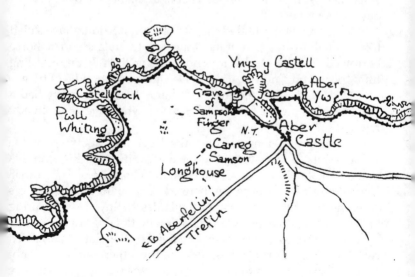

Folklore and The Early Celtic Saints

So far, we have described features of the area, historically verifiable facts about Porthgain and the district around, and what to do to enjoy it.

But there are other historical details which are less factual, as one understands the term today. This is not to say that the tales are invented but rather that accretion of details which are legendary became attached to a small kernel of fact.

South-West Wales and the St David's area in particular were of great moment in the days of the early Christian Celtic church, fifteen hundred years ago when St David and his fellow wandering monks were active, and travelling between Brittany, Ireland, Cornwall and Wales in their primitive craft.

St David's mother has a connection with Llanon, a tiny hamlet east of Llanrhian. At the hour of David's birth, St Non pressed her hands on a stone which retained the imprints and it may be that this stone is an ogam stone beneath the altar of an ancient chapel at Llanon about a mile to the east of Llanrhian church, although of course the place of St David's birth is traditionally associated with the tiny ruined chapel in the field above St Non's Bay, just south of St David's.

St Finbarre, who founded the city of Cork is said to have sailed from Traethllwyn. And if he travelled to Ireland on a horse borrowed from St David, it is no stranger than St Piran sailing from Ireland on a mill-stone or St Decumen on a bundle of twigs.

St Cadoc, too, is associated with Barry Island where he had a cell; and what are we to make of Samson, whom we have already referred to?

But even more unusual than the legendary activities of the Celtic saints is an account quoted by Sir John Rhys in his monumental volumes on Celtic Folklore. This relates how in 1858 Daniel Huws was journeying between Fishguard and St David's when he saw, off Trefin, one of the ladies of Rhys Ddwfn sitting on a stone while she disentangled her long flowing silvery hair.

While she was performing her toilette, the slate quarrymen (whether from Porthgain or one of the other quarries is not specified) went down to investigate and when they got near they

perceived that, from her waist upwards she was a woman but from her waist downwards she had the body of a fish.

When they talked to her, she replied in Welsh, though the only words she uttered were 'Reaping in Pembrokeshire, and weeding in Carmarthenshire." And back she went into the sea, her home.

Another mermaid was seen off Llanwnda and yet another at Aberbach, both on the edge of our area.

There was also a tradition around 1850 among the inhabitants of Trefin, that from Llanon could be seen, out at sea, the Green Islands of the Deep.

Normally speaking, the Green Isles were invisible but they could be seen under special circumstances. If you took a turf from St David's churchyard and stood on it on the seashore, you could see the islands. And there was also the local tradition here that they could be seen from Llanon.

The traditions of Y Tylwyth Teg, the Fair Family or Fairies are well documented on this peninsula and were widely believed until last century. Round here they were also called Plant Rhys Ddwfn – the Children of Rhys the Deep (meaning wise or cunning); and they lived on the Green Isles of the Deep. The relationship between them and the mermaids does not seem to be clearly defined anywhere unfortunately.

In the booklet on Myths and Legends of Wales, in this series, there is more detail about the inhabitants of the Green Isles and their way of life.

And, if this seems to us a curiously intangible way to end a booklet concerned with the factual past and present, it would not have done so to our ancestors a hundred years or more ago.